favorite maritime drinking songs of the miraculous alcoholics

favorite maritime drinking songs of the miraculous alcoholics

*poems by
Matt Schumacher*

Wild Man of the Woods Press

First Trade Paperback Edition

No part of this publication may be reproduced, stored or transmitted in any form or by any means, electronic, mechanical, photocopying, recording, scanning, or otherwise without written permission from the publisher. It is illegal to copy this book, post it to a website, or distribute it by any other means without permission.

ISBN: 979-8-9930162-6-9

Text © 2026 by Matt Schumacher

Editor and Publisher, Justin T. O'Conor Sloane
Cover art: *Kraken's Lair* © 2026 by Bob Eggleton
Book design by F. J. Bergmann

Wild Man of the Woods Press

an imprint of Starship Sloane Publishing Company, Inc.
Austin–Round Rock, Texas
starshipsloane.com

Table of Contents

dionysia

a dionysian outburst	3
drinking song	4
a drunk driving lesson with the miraculous alcoholics	5
les alcooliques miraculeux et le bateau ivre	6
drinking song for loaded poets	7
song of satyrnalian mirth	8
they caper like the satyrs	9
a great deal of kicking up one's heels	10
the miraculous alcoholics look sleek and composed	11
the miraculous alcoholics drink the great lakes	12
why they drink deep	13
incomprehensibly thirsty	14
festive pastimes of the miraculous alcoholics	15
should auld acquaintance be forgot	16
a thirst as legendary as their exploits	17
non-anonymously, the miraculous alcoholics unanimously	19
drunken coronation	20
the kings of spilled drinks	21
malt liquor anthem	22
their tossing ships	23
less miraculous alcoholics	24

black suns, dystopias, and dry counties

perilously liquefied in so liquid an era	27
cocktails crow like roosters	28

the miraculous alcoholics slip you the keys to the speakeasy	29
they concoct unorthodox drinks	30
they sip the drink they've christened	31
they infuse dry lives with liquid verse	32
they enchant the pantheon	33
towering folklore of their overpowering thirst	34
will the miraculous alcoholics drink it all?	35
they brandish glasses abrim with absinthe	36
the miraculous alcoholics crash saturnine soirées	37
all hail the alcoholic kings of icebergs	38
the miraculous alcoholics just unleashed	39

miracles

miraculous backwards abecedarius recited for police	43
they revive dead rivertowns	44
like bold, luckless etruscan pirates	45
when the miraculous alcoholics throw a party	47
the miraculous alcoholics retrieve last evening piece by piece	48
the miraculous alcoholics liquefy their lives	49
"a vast sea where there is nothing but the abode of monsters"	50
lost at sea	51
asked why they drink every drink in sight, they reply	52
they tip over niagara falls	53
they breach lake okeechobee	54
a flaskful of inebriated magistrates	55
they steer ghost ships into watering holes	56
they drink spring's return	57

afterworlds

the miraculous alcoholics free all the world behind bars	61
the miraculous alcoholics leap into the past to shoot free pool	62
they sip mesopotamian epics	63
the miraculous alcoholics steal ideal sweetness	64
they go drinking with villon	65
with a hellish splash	66
their legend grows as they cultivate bliss	67
liquid mountaineers	68
lightning bottleworks	69
they plunder wonderland	70
the miraculous alcoholics mix the apocalypse	71
with a universe of galaxies all elixirs	72
sea reverie	73
epilogue	74
notes	77
acknowledgments	79
about the author	81

Bacchus pours out wine for a panther, while Silenus plays the lyre, painting from Boscoreale, Campania, c. 30 BC (British Museum)

dionysia

Either through the influence of narcotic drink, of which all primitive men and peoples speak, or through the powerful coming on of spring, which drives joyfully through all of nature, that Dionysian excitement arises. Under the magic of the Dionysian, not only does the bond between man and man lock itself in place once more, but also nature itself, no matter how alienated, hostile, or subjugated, rejoices again in her festival of reconciliation with her prodigal son, man. The earth freely offers up her gifts, and the beasts of prey from the rocks and the desert approach in peace.

—Nietzsche

a dionysian outburst

the miraculous alcoholics drink the *reckless swashbuckler*
and blastoff from a shotglass, on the prowl
to sip what waitress calls the *howling wolverine*,
or powerlift the tavern's best, *the headless schwarzenegger*,
or ride whatever bartender serves, even the *surfer on acid*.
revived by *barracuda bite* and *abracadabra*,
they outlast the *beautiful disaster*, imbibe the *unbridled unicorn*,
reap all the liquid pleasures of the *terror from the deep*
and the *twenty thousand leagues under the sea*.
they sneak tangerine iced tea
like liquor ripped off from paradise,
keep mysteriously spiked steins of a drink
known only as the *eugene dangerous* close by.
they deck their halls with christmas-tree-water martinis
until carols leak from every barroom seam.
they reach extreme circus tent ceilings of glee,
shot out of the rocket of a cocktail called *tarzan of the trapeze*.
they brave the wolfsbane, soar aloof due to the *ufo in a typhoon*,
drink lakefuls of the *moonquake shake*,
direct bartenders to postpone taxi cab,
for they must be served a drink reserved for them,
the *inverted traffic light*. they end where they begin,
shotglassed by a mad belfryful of bats,
and land miraculously asleep, three sheets to the bedspins.

drinking song

the miraculous alcoholics think
boozed-up snobs and yuppie fops
less festive party guests than cops.
cops, at least, shout and start, wave guns,
flail frantic at bacchanalian antics.
such bourgeois duds, such punks
smug as fuck, could put them in a slump.
champagne be damned. slammed pabst
spiked by 151. blurred vision forcefed thunderbird
until bedspins send them churning to the head.
better yet, send them on beer runs to bad neighborhoods.
tap the last keg, that glistening beast of foam,
oceans of gushing suds, tidal pint after pint—
that rainstorm in their throats, sloshing its way home.

a drunk driving lesson with the miraculous alcoholics

when the miraculous alcoholics gun their engines
and drag race the wrong way on a one way,
their arms and legs suggesting street signs need to be revised,
police agree their impaired motor skills provide more thrilling
   rides
and are so happy for them, especially as they take air over
   bumps
in the backwoods or hills, they issue no DUIS.
it's a miracle they're still alive, the way they're swilling
vodka, gin, whiskey and vermouth, their garage
a bottle collage, a private liquor store. boozed
up dipsomaniacs, reckless from kalamazoo to duluth,
no small miracle it is they find their way home at night.
what nerve they have to whoop out loud,
honking at the cops, swerving with delight.

Matt Schumacher

les alcooliques miraculeux et le bateau ivre

> And from that time on I bathed in the Poem
> Of the Sea, star-infused and churned into milk,
> Devouring the green azures; where, entranced in pallid flotsam,
> A dreaming drowned man sometimes goes down;
>
> —Rimbaud, "The Drunken Boat"

because the poem of the sea inebriates,
they pilot the terrible child's own drunken boat,
shipwreck that cares nothing for its crew.
they harvest phosphorescence from the darkest waters
with black sea horse escorts
bridled by lightning from furious clouds,
sip the sweet hiss of twisting waterspout,
devour the green azures of the dreaming drowned,
pass whole seasons in hells pellucid and hallucinatory.
they meet the eye of leviathan.
their cutlassed drunkenness will bleed all the colors of coral
    reefs,
and rise like iridescent pirates from fata morgana.
it will place their thirst in delicate quarantine.
braced for glacier, lured by icebergs,
shackled to oblivion aboard ships of fools,
aloof as the mistral, they breathe through aquamarine lungs.
lost siren pearls appear in their ears.
doubloons from the depths balance on their tongues.

drinking song for loaded poets

dry bards try hard cider,
wax lyrical when liquified.
parched scops stoop to gut rot.
lax scribes imbibe the wiles of ales and wines.
bored, out of sorts troubadours
cavort after one snort of port.
sad balladeers' ballads brim with cheer
when they swallow tall gallon beers.
metallurgists wisely hide quicksilver
from the notice of mercurial poets
who'd pilfer any liquid sliver.
laureates in a rut
can't keep liquor cabinets shut.
curses or burps interrupt their best lines.
immersed verses turn lush
as stashes and stanzas get ambushed.
morose sonneteers lunch
on spiked everclear punch.
stammering wordsmiths laggard
with thirst liquefy, and skewer the worst
verse, banish their own inner
verbose, banal windbags.
hammered poets pen homeric epics.

Matt Schumacher

song of satyrnalian mirth

the miraculous alcoholics turn pub crawl into maul ball,
those sallow louts who brawl longer than law allows.
surely they carouse with such blush-faced gusto
god cannot bless these thuggish drunks any less
than he blesses young amish ruffians,
stomping at barn hops during rumspringa,
or jack mormons, wide-eyed on LSD instead of LDS.
irrationality makes sense. slaves invert
aristocratic worlds forever into carnivalesque.
as satyrs sow wild oats, half drunken man,
half bowled-over goat,
these winos fly to dionysian heights,
soar over castle moats,
caper, then leap clean
over every last pastoral shepherd's fence.

favorite maritime drinking songs of the miraculous alcoholics

they caper like the satyrs

> *or let a noble vintage slosh over the rim of the barrel*
> *on the heights of Vesuvius as the satyrs lead the dance …*
> —Marcel Detienne

their beatific leaps unseat despots
whose absolute rule after their liquid coup
merely means free vodka shots.
the stoic chagrined stand and cheer
to see them ascend yet again:
such leaps beseech barkeeps
for beers as tall as ceilings,
plead to reach some gravity-free equilibrium.
as euripedean earthquake leaped,
obliterating theban castle, barroom restrooms
reverberate with ancient laughter.
the leaping leaks they take connect to cosmic streams:
in porcelain turned to olden wine bowl,
vesuvian yellows bubble into
the bearded, blissful face of some great satyr,
right foot raised for revelry,
reaching the zenith of his caper from a far age:
cackling back at us, ecstatic bacchus
bounds to boundless godhood on olympus.

a great deal of kicking up one's heels

lacking dance partners, the miraculous alcoholics
skip the prom and gallivant with their bad habits,
plastered, blasted, tripping lights fantastic.
barroom rather than ballroom ballerinas,
they lean and twirl like elixirs aswirl
as their hips spin like stirred and shaken gin and tonics.
something between a mashed potato and a human torpedo
is born on dancefloors of their own intoxication.
they drink until they sink all ships asail
in tall, icy glasses, until their kossack kicks
thaw white russian siberias.
what moves might bust loose,
what strange dances might transpire, bouncer,
bartender, and police have no idea.
the limes they bite lead inevitably to more tequila.

the miraculous alcoholics look sleek and composed

as a cold mezcal bottle in the midday desert shadows.
composed when propped aghast in bathroom stalls,
sleek while slurring words before tall glasses,
immersed in rare aguardiente,
they seem to live forever at some far oasis.
they make sunstroke their pillow,
mirage their odd bedfellow.
someone who overhears them unzipping spines,
as they disrobe from saguaro suit, and undo
heavy aloe vera boots,
please distill into morphine drip
the ease that spreads when they slip on opium pajamas.
deliver their valerian nightclothes.
let us slumber like them with one hand on the motherlode
like b. traven, or ambrose bierce,
purposefully lost and known only by aliases in mexico.

the miraculous alcoholics drink the great lakes

the miraculous alcoholics are tipsy from oconomowoc
    to poughkeepsie,
for every heave of the sea, from boom to lee, is lost
on these gloating stowaways,
these shot-to-hell sailors, soaked with dripping chasers.
look at their drinks swirling like nautilus shells.
their ferries merrily trolling the great lakes of bar and tavern,
slaking thirsts as multifarious as flathead catfish whiskers.
most slowly they drink, the way toothless spoonbills
scoop plankton, but when they capture their second wind,
their chartered steamboats and drunk captain
    startle the harbor.
when the miraculous alcoholics deem to put on
    their captain nemo routine,
the bartender's submerged as a drunken jules verne.
he leaves the bar open as michigan, superior, huron, and erie.

favorite maritime drinking songs of the miraculous alcoholics

why they drink deep

*the rest wander among men as numberless sorrows,
since earth and sea teem with miseries.*

—Hesiod

to sink like krill in a baleen
and swirl down to the unseen,
diving bell the belly of blue whale,
framed by the eye of bigfin squid.
to be some terrible thing poseidon did.
to binge until unhinged since hope's shut in
its sunken box. to lubricate the hoary jail locks
and take a drink to drown out each
of earth and sea's unseemly, teeming miseries.
to, like lotus eaters, live lives swallowed whole.
to, like cyclops eyes, down worlds in a single gulp.
for legend or lore like corroded copper ore
portends neverending benders
that turn men green. to dream cold seeps
and sultry hydrothermal vents.
to absorb stores of transformed spirits,
flitting fermentations, benthic bubbles bent transparent.
to show as many shiny, shifting forms as proteus.
to try the might of triton's storms.
to wake up as drowned as a coastal town
halfslain by hurricane
and not be dead. to be consoled by haloes
bursting across surfaces, their eyelids oceans,
bioluminescences glimpsed high above their heads.
to know waves throw every drop they have at them,
as if hoping that they'll sink. this world's
like an endless kegger, begging them to drink.

incomprehensibly thirsty

sires of full pints flirt with frightful splurge
only to lure servers into the absurd:
like kaspar hausers, half-wild, wolf-child howlers'
doused mouths won't pronounce a word.
spilling hard sarsparilla, befuddled sluggards
chug suds, slur and curse. barbaric martian bards
mar mahogany bars like loose, toothful alligator gar.
stungunned lushes like drunk bums
slog through froth and mash, flushed and mum,
drink, dash, and slash all slushfunds.
charlatans clearly chant when out of earshot,
smashing wits to bits can be such roguish fun!
when mushmouthed gushers stumble into dumps
and slap the bar for more like humpbacked whales'
thunderclaps assail cold atlantic waters,
fearful barmen rush to satisfy their wants.

festive pastimes
of the miraculous alcoholics

the miraculous alcoholics spool whirlpools
and spin them on their hips like hulahoops,
whereupon they appear to be drowning.
slack as kraken, they're the type rumored to mutiny,
hands daft as masts, blasted captains, dabbling damned ahabs.
their every revolution circumscribes bermuda triangles,
to hear them tell it, as they recline, dangling legs
over ship railings like the skinniest of fishing poles.
sinfully drinking flips and swinging eggnogs,
a coastguard of poltroons, mugs foaming with rumfustian,
albatross tossed into the sea, unsold on omens,
spies to the last man, rebelliously seeing right through
the veritable spyglass of piracy.

should auld acquaintance be forgot

the miraculous alcoholics will buy your friendship with a shot.
then they'll renovate new year's eve,
fill the glasses of the feral underclasses.
beer-soaked musketeers, they'll veer
into revolutionary spheres:
they'll bow after starting a row
and raise a fracas,
in the noisemaking name
of shitfaced bacchus.
they'll kidnap dick clark,
and make him dance drunk and naked,
skyscrapered atop the empire state.
snockered kropotkins with the conscience
of missiles, knocking down restroom stalls,
stealing keys to the city
from scared mayor and pissing officials,
they'll take control like untrained crane operators
whose swinging demolition machines
smash times square crystal to smithereens.
they'll drop their shangri-la
like a whiskey-filled wrecking ball,
declare a valhalla of free alcohol for all.

favorite maritime drinking songs of the miraculous alcoholics

a thirst as legendary as their exploits

> *his feats were many, his exploits endless,*
> *and his thirst legendary.*
>
> —back label of a bottle of Captain Morgan Spiced Rum

here's to their drinking spree, their unbelievable bender.
the brokendown liquor cabinet door.
the nervous convenience store clerks.
the devastated booze in walk-in coolers. the blender.
they'll drink the kitchen sink, the skating rink,
the whiskey river, the river otter's private stash,
the monster vat of sour mash, the glasses of those
passed out at the all-night bash, the anger
of wine store owners who must chase them
away from obliterated wine-tastings.
they'll slurp the foam like sots sampling the flotsam,
immuring themselves in luxurious froth.
they'll wrestle waterfalls and jump off the raft in laughter
in an effort to swallow all the whitewater.
they'll drown down the dandelion wine and all the formal cordials,
warn fathers to hide away their sons and daughters,
chug beers of those indisposed in restrooms.
they'll quaff whatever spills into log flume
then demand to ride an iceberg to greenland or the aleutian isles.
they'll eagerly huff the gasoline in your garage
and raid the mini-refrigerator's week-old gatorade.
they'd drink a year's worth of trade with southeast asia.
they'd jump through brewery vat hoops like orcas.
they're the vampire bats to your wild orchids,
delicate hummingbirds sucking hibiscus.
they'll drink your science experiment and its meniscus,

Matt Schumacher

leave you wondering where the lid is,
dare you toward the everclear stood-up hair of the rottweiler.
before they're finished, dionysus himself will buy them a guinness.
they'll gulp down the spiked christmas punch just for fun,
polish off whatever drops into abandoned party hat,
rip open empty twelve packs and ransack cans for last sips.
their boozy radar, however, should not be confused for stupor.
they'll drink the past and future,
but are interested in a drink first thing this morning
to rebound from a rocky combination
of cottonmouth, ditchweed, and mandarin orange vodka.

non-anonymously, the miraculous alcoholics unanimously

vote until they elect themselves the true lords of misrule.
renegade bootleggers, oblivious to blue laws,
they who champion drinking games
behind enemy dry-county lines,
posing riddles, throwing dice.
they ply police with hard lemonade and breezer,
see that each teetotaler's fitted with beer goggles.
they disbelieve in boggled mind, blackout, or seizure,
these stowaways slipped safely aboard
the gallant ship they call *drunkenness*,
longshoremen whose foremen have long ago
forsworn wharf for bar,
oarsmen who've traded oars for yards of ale.
they navigate by stars seen after barroom fights,
toward horizons momentarily aligned,
running until still, from bahamian rum
to appalachian moonshine.

drunken coronation

> It is not for kings to drink wine.
> —Proverbs 31:4

on barstool thrones and booths
the miraculous alcoholics crown themselves
the kings of alehouses and distilleries.
they're the type that were barrel pilloried
when swilling was still villainy.
their slurred, inebriated speech
like mutterings of interrupted sleep.
see them preen like impeached presidents
in grief. their impaired balance almost a stance,
a shambling, poorly coordinated dance.
their flushed faces and red eyes ashamed
brighten for a moment after
disorderly households' euphoric outbursts.
these drunken kings tap kegs, slap casks,
legislate and disperse unlawfully tall glasses,
hang like unwieldy, hammered chandeliers,
like cackling falstaffs from the rafters.

the kings of spilled drinks

keep spilling drinks all over themselves,
and all over everyone else,
on some clumsy, cataclysmic binge,
until hydrology can't slow alluvial flow:
immersing the premises until waitress must row,
until seep means swamp, and leads to flood,
until gin drenching the skin
rivals that in the blood,
and bleary-eyed helmsmen can not steer,
until barstools used as water wheels
mill and brew free beer,
these rightful kings leak whiskey creeks,
surf spilled pilsner goldrush
and aqueductal flux,
slip into deliquium.
afloat on foam, soaked in estuary,
dipped in sloe gin inlets to the toes,
they flush their heads forgetful and clean
in sluice of vodka and grapefruit juice,
evolve rivulet and venetian canal
to solve mouthfuls of drought.
these vassals amass vast washed away castles
and ride their own overflowing kingdoms to freedom.

malt liquor anthem

the miraculous alcoholics fault malt liquor for their troubles,
the way wasted revelers may blame
champagne for all its bubbles.
ridiculously blitzed on schlitz,
or snakebitten by king cobra,
pissed and amiss on olde english,
booze cheaper than club soda,
these soused and lousy houseguests,
plowed on mickey's big mouths,
disenfranchised by bad frog or evil eye,
nonetheless hoist the heightened alcohol of forty ounces high:
they lift it toward the sky to cloud their judgment,
tip it for revelry, buoyancy, and lightened soul,
they open mouths to praise this yellow scapegoat,
the drink of necessity for homeless, and unemployed,
and polish off its golden malted liquor whole.

favorite maritime drinking songs of the miraculous alcoholics

their tossing ships

> *on this more traditional view, the self was to be regarded as an enormous whisky vat, in which experiences fermented quietly until they were mellow and mature.*
>
> —Terry Eagleton, *How to Read a Poem*

the miraculous alcoholics capture and tap
    the enormous whisky vat
of the self, their dilated blood vessels, their staggering gait.
evading the brightwork, leaping athwartships,
their revelry, loutish yet stalwart, plaits
tradition with dangerous irrationality,
that reckless sedan of a catamaran
named the death of man. it's true
pilots absorb booze more rapidly
at high altitudes, their livers tall castles
of milkthistle, but goats and louts half
sunk in stouts and moats,
peering out english murder holes
to shout *who knows where
there's beer,* or filled to
the brim with toasts,
might be true poet poltroons,
sloshed neptunes, tridentless,
allowing our subterranean,
previously unheard-of selves
fluency, music, crisp exactitudes.

less miraculous alcoholics

maybe pray to the necessary saints,
for today, they're weeping statues.
st. philomena, remove their noose
or fire a flare for angels.
hubert of liege, patron saint of mad dogs,
pray they stay sane and stop chasing their tails.
st. jude, patron of lost causes,
greatly acquainted with derailed trains,
show them ways to replace sorrow
with grace, how to wait for desperation to fade.
monica, patron saint of alcoholics,
the present engulfs them
faster than they blink, much less finish a first drink.
dominic savio, you who died at fifteen,
patron saint of juvenile delinquents,
feel free to more frequently intervene,
please persuade them to leave
before a sober patron calls the police.
some modern moses is needed to lead,
to cleave these meaningless seas
which cast them adrift further from home,
until they're derelict relics
that dimly recollect their former selves,
livers afflicted with sickness.
st. nicholas, patron of shipwrecks,
listen when they plead *forgive us. we're lost
sailors, landlocked, but hellishly sinking.
drink is a sea that teaches mermaids to weep,
a sea which leads us so deep within ourselves
we've no recourse but to continue drinking.*

black suns, dystopias, and dry counties

The thirsty *Earth* soaks up the *Rain*,
And drinks, and gapes for drink again.
The *Plants* suck in the *Earth*, and are
With constant drinking fresh and faire.
The *Sea* itself, which one would think
Should have but little need of *Drink*,
Drinks ten thousand *Rivers* up,
So fill'd that they oreflow the *Cup*.
The busie *Sun* (and one would guess)
By's drunken firy face no less)
Drinks up the *Sea*, and when 'has don,
The *Moon* and *Stars* drink up the *Sun*.

—Anacreon (tr. Cowley)

perilously liquefied in so liquid an era

with the limitless thirst of the present,
they drink liquid modernity.
fading waitresses haunt their table
with unstable, opaque cocktails,
fateful glasses of precarious uncertainty.
jaded protagonists on the ropes of dystopias,
post-panoptical modern nomads,
vengeful fluid druids who dissolve stonehenge,
on the ledge of a binge,
they hesitate at the pale glint of precipitate,
witness the faint hiss of dissolution.
taken aback by the lack of traction,
the absence of visible solid edge
and tangible shape in the modern age,
the gestalt of their debts, they must settle
into the unsettled life of a miraculous alcoholic:
exiled, exterritorial, insolite.

cocktails crow like roosters

and hold new orleans jazz funerals
in the miraculous alcoholics' hands.
bloody marys put on crimson spats,
twirl scarlet pirouettes,
hurl flugelhorns at the hungover
like scary, cathartic marching bands.
hot toddies, scalding odysseys,
brand the throat. grasshoppers
seethe with real, long-legged liquid insects
who feast on thirst in mint julep jackets.
kamikazes shred and spear
dead dive tavern atmospheres with fizz.
surfers on acid gloat, float on violet tidal waves
into weary bars. zombies rise to buy you beers.
raucous drink orders buzz.
boozehounds croon like drunk tank karaoke.

the miraculous alcoholics slip you the keys to the speakeasy

slinking into dark backrooms,
sinking into booths, sunk in
on a ruthless, 100-proof
campaign to dampen temperance,
they sneak keys to lucky souls like you,
then sport the house a round
of corpse revivers to
get the roaring twenties roaring drunk
and count survivors.
why not ply whiskey on the sly
as glasses slosh and slide
from same drawer in the wall
money was slid into?
why not consign one's thirst
to blind tigers where drinkers on a mission
drown mouths parched from prohibition,
after whispered passwords, secret handshakes?
why not help themselves
take drink-all-you-like bartending lessons
and sidesaddle up in the horse latitudes
of cloudy double vision?
why not retreat from temperate streets
down hidden stairways stumbled on
by lucky guesses, where
bouncy jazz and bootleg moonshine
lead to jitterbugging sheiks
and shimmyings of flappers' sleeveless dresses?

they concoct unorthodox drinks

preparing to consume the *moonshine truly from the moon*
or whipping up the *tippling, looselipped sphinx,*
they boldly propose preposterous potions
as if they'd siphoned the sky for the mix,
stood the great pyramid of cheops on its very tip to fix them.
swaggering gallants, staggering into balance,
fix such flips and slings presidents must,
with liquor cabinets, staff oval offices.
like cocktails spiked with live water moccasins,
their slick elixirs slither to the last dry patron.
they have the nerve to pry open private reserves
like slaves unafraid to raid
and loot pharoah's hoarded stores.
corks, screw tops, and more
take flight like sudden snowball fights
among the plowed. bottle tops pop off,
aloft like shooting stars
into the oohing, aahing crowd.
reports of their molotovs
bring the fire department to the bar.
the miraculous alcoholics must take action:
the coup called cooler beverages,
sconce and tankard for the cops,
liquefaction.

they sip the drink they've christened

wanderlust in fits and gusts
while ashambles with chablis blush,
then reveal to everyone
this tall glass of squall
is the pure recklessness of it all
whispering in a seashell.
it tastes of waves crashing on your rocks.
its smashed bubbles against your hull
send you sailing round the world.
whatever they sip brings them rapture
with the travelogue of the four winds,
sends them on endless adventures
just beginning, leaves them
with eyes contrived by sunset's golden light,
captures some farflung dalliance
with the hesperides. to the pure rush
of exhilarations, raise a stein.
here's to the miraculous alcoholics.
here's to proof-through-the-roof,
torrential good times.

they infuse dry lives with liquid verse

Enjoy your life,
for you're a long time dead.

—Scottish proverb

who knew medieval brutes would thatch roofs
then beat down the doors to be troubadours,
plucking lutes attuned to such fluid music?
who knew crude poltroons could restore truth,
leaving harsh barrooms so melodiously ludic?
the miraculous alcoholics knew all along
life might pass by quite dry without drinking songs,
might deprive lifetimes of fizz and bite,
leave the dry exiled on an isle with no gusto.
therefore, their songs roust spirit from the dust,
slay the raging hangovers' pall, as they must,
bow and flow toward the lowly,
retrieve our squandered aqua vitae.
they may raise oases on desiccated days.
thus, their hiccups kick up a ruckus:
behold these knights who belch pure chivalry.

favorite maritime drinking songs of the miraculous alcoholics

they enchant the pantheon

what audacity! crashing that party at mt. olympus
with a twelve pack of olympia just to hand one cheap beer
to each of the greek gods! and to fool zeus with the shaken can!
who do these miraculous alcoholics think they are?
booms juno, laughing so hard she's in tears.
apollo cries, *more beer! no more charioteer!*
i'll let a taraxippus take my reins if this fiesta lasts all night.
they lure and soothe the furies with alcoholic slurries,
curry mars' contrary favor with maraschino liqueur.
prometheus overreaches yet still can't hold a candle to their
    rising star.
they sweettalk hermes into being their designated flyer,
promising to do handstands in his sandals,
yelling *see you in hell* at doomsday's lord, hades.
their impression dawns upon aurora
and especially allures the minds of divine ladies:
artemis approves the moon as far-flung, canary yellow barroom,
lunar nightclub where gravity-free stags chase and darts levitate.
birthed from the sea far less memorably than botticelli's venus,
their messy selves bloom, dutifully groomed by beauty's goddess.
breaking flawless laws, they stir minerva's very thinking cap
    to awe:
sinking straws into immortal seas,
they swirl eternity like a fresh drink.

towering folklore
of their overpowering thirst

everywhere the miraculous alcoholics are
it's open bar. and it may well take
a good part of the great lakes,
may suck dry aqueducts,
break and burst dams,
to slake their unquenchable thirst
just sitting at your average dive bar,
drinking schlitz and hamms.
they may frolic their way through yards
of beer, hoist so many tall highballs,
so many strong cognac tonics,
the evening may stumble in soaked to the socks,
may yet involve fluid hydraulics.
the bar may float off like a barge
and their thirst will be forced
to fire a flare to shore for a lifeboat.
they've declared monsoon season for their desert throats.
there's lightning dancing in their thunderheads.
authorities report *they're well out of hand.*
and their thirst, bowlegged outlaw,
sidles into the saloon like the only reason
to hold all drinks ransom
and list endless demands.

will the miraculous alcoholics drink it all?

with smiles wider than beer aisles.
such a thirst assails their brains
they deem themselves able to drink whole worlds of ales.
they'll leave telltale trails of empties.
they'll divine the many worlds they drink by signs
like blind drunks delighted to stumble
on their own kind of braille.
they'll drink until the ditches cry
and the rivers heave dry sighs,
until the lakes crawl away afraid
and the deserts buy the thirstcrazed drinks.
they'll drink primitively in caves
and drink into existence the modern age.
they'll drink tomorrow. and they'll drink today.
they may accidentally swallow a small town,
and what's more, may guzzle entire reservoirs.
they'll drink cheaply, and at great cost.
they'll drink in palace and stall.
until home feels like home.
until whole civilizations are lost.
100 bottles of beer on the wall
have never seemed a number so small
when ruthless thirsts greet suds this voluminous.
who's unafraid to drink all the world's beer?
the miraculous alcoholics raise their hands as eager volunteers,
click glasses, and rousingly say *cheers*

they brandish glasses abrim with absinthe

they believe they're deepsea divers
diving on dry land. delirium tremens,
they claim, inflicts them with the bends.
like toulouse-lautrec, they contend
such afflictions may only be relieved
by illicitly distilled, illegal
sea-green psychotropic drinks.
they feign surprise when warned one sip
may mean overdoses, hospital trips.
psychiatric therapy reverts to absinthe drips.
liquor bottles glint, widen into bars aglow
inside their artemisia crystal balls
until it's difficult to think. soon
they're so far lost in the wormwoods
their lush forest can furnish no response.
Shhh ... our hushed narration mustn't disturb their buzz.
due to cube, peculiar liquid, slotted spoon,
yes, a highly pleasurable absentia has set in
as spirits precipitate under glass,
about to float and defy the dead.
behold as liquid magic lantern shows unfold
under opalescent louche moon:
see wilde, rimbaud, baudelaire, van gogh
raise glasses, gloat and toast the greenest fairy,
coquettishly batting her eyelashes
as their drunken boat's emerald figurehead.

the miraculous alcoholics crash saturnine soirées

I am saturnine—bereft—disconsolate,
The Prince of Aquitaine whose tower has crumbled;
My lone star is dead—and my bespangled lute
Bears the Black Sun of Melancholia.

—Gérard de Nerval

they infuse the black sun of melancholia
with moonwhitened dew and liquid blooming magnolia,
promenade nerval's lobster along la rue des lunatiques,
stir mercutio's mirth into hamlet's glass,
assure listless ladies and morose lords have a blast.
wildly abnormal at the formal dance,
they convince brooding princes of gloom
to slam the spiked milk of cows jumping over the moon.
they invigorate mouldering castle and crypt
with casks of spirited imperial stout.
brisk with whiskey, up and about,
dumping abundant smuggler's rum
into punchbowl from puncture-proof jugs,
these blokes with no control move ghouls to laughter
with hip flask and whispered joke.
though death stares them down,
rift and trench drown in their rippling, infectious fits.
they drip bliss into abyss, and titillate hell itself.
falling down drunk in the waves,
they flail until the sea's belly trembles and swells.

all hail the alcoholic kings of icebergs

truly miraculous booze refuses to freeze.
frigid research concludes antarctic icebergs sing
like humming beehives or shrill violins
when water navigates its tunnels and ravines.
like winter lowering the boom, our heroes
regale alehouse with iceberg serenades.
they wait as these frozen behemoths plait labrador's straits.
pale glacial nomads awakened from a far land
of perpetual shade stare ahead. their cold gaze
reflects hypnos' grasp, lethe's forgetfulness.
thawed from the hoarfrost jaws of hinterlands,
from tundras whose sole residents are frozen to death,
most at home with pinnacle and dome
as if calved from greenland's western coast,
with loud voices from beyond the north wind
they point out their poisonous choices,
hoisting three-foot icicles broken off the bar roof.
boastful barbarians brandishing ice swords,
revealing truths of arctic sleuths,
lords of the cold half-threaten, half-shout
ordering drinks with this fjord spar
must earn me free eisbocks in this ice shelf of a bar
for at least the next three evenings!

the miraculous alcoholics
just unleashed

the longest piss in the world.
taking leaks like thoroughbreds at preakness stakes,
they lean back, let these ceaseless jetstreams fly
so long lovers forget each other's lies,
and those so long in coiled lines place bets....

yes, so long sunbeams turn to moonbeams,
daydreams climb right into night dreams,
kids learn alphabets, and old folks number their regrets.
for a time, the entire world gleams as if
merely their yo-yo on a yellow liquid string.
they find they're half in disbelief.
never mind the grief, the gravity of things—
why not laugh? yet it's that sigh
escaping afterward that's best:
yes, the blissful finish, that satisfaction
foreverafter called complete relief.

miracles

The world man knows, the world in which he has settled himself so securely and snugly—that world is no more. The turbulence which accompanied the arrival of Dionysus has not been transformed into a charming fairy story or into an ingenuous child's paradise. The primeval world has stepped into the foreground, the depths of reality have opened, the elemental forms of everything that is creative, everything that is destructive, have arisen, bringing with them infinite rapture and infinite terror.

—Walter F. Otto, from *Dionysus, Myth and Cult*

miraculous backward abecedarius recited for police

zeroing in on the ouzo, these
yeast-soused roustabouts whose labors of ale are revelry,
x-ed out of their minds on boxed wine, like
wharf rats stowed inside puncheons of rum,
vermouthed to the tooth,
urinating on no trespassing signs,
tremblement de terre'd,
surrender to rapidly shifting mood.
raiders blackstrapped,
quizzically liquored to the boots,
picaresque drinkers, jousting with windowsills,
oscillating on barstools, compasses used to
navigate, to weave whiskeyed streams.
malted crusaders,
lapping rapturously
krausened beers,
jubilantly
infused with inebriants, they
hector slime and ooze into nectar. such
guzzlers grow
flabbergasted on dubious punch.
ecstatic as if lightning were their sombrero,
dram-slamming
curanderos
brandish as many arms as an octopus
and tip a drink up in each one.

Matt Schumacher

they revive dead rivertowns

> *Bourbon is corn liquor*
> *with a college education.*
> —Sterling Brown

o ebullient fools
who flood whole towns with good times,
you miraculous alcoholics,
high in the still-riddled hills
by glorious moonshine
you admired your old,
swollen, low valley abodes.
you heard ditchwater whisper,
drown your former lives.
lungs slung with field hollers and arhoolies,
bones breath-filled hollows,
you glowed gold as all louisiana's saxophones.
your mouths shouted downpours,
melting mississippi deltas.
you spilled sloughs bruised with gutbucket blues,
salve that healed cheated ladies
and redeemed abandoned gentlemen.
now you bring such shindig and fling
dead rivertowns swear revelry spreads as do tsunamis.
your mardi gras embarks like teeming beasts
from steamboat noah's arks.
your floodwaters leave fluviatile fields
fertile crescents of concupiescence.
your firkins free meadowlarks.
you make listless shacks cackle like palatial jackals
until, with bliss, each bad castle sings.
you pour such satisfying, sparkling drinks
whole bars agree there must be a god.

like bold, luckless etruscan pirates

the miraculous alcoholics mistakenly abduct dionysus.
the spindrift spray and wreckage of their days
washed away in waves by thalassa,
they find charybdis is the liquid child of madness.
gazing into whirlpool-eyed stare, they're dared
by siren choirs to pour the afternoon down their throats.
tentacled to their first drink, blinding *libri fulgurales*.
sails laden with grapes larger than men's heads.
by the gods, go back, or we'll all be dead!
the boy's a sorcerer! their helmsman warns.
with minds like ahabs, captainswheels flee their craft.
sobriety's fast mangled in a panther's fangs and claws.
frenzy has no laws: their oars turn to serpents,
writhing in their fists, striking at their eyes,
frightening them overboard. a horde of shapes,
a nightmare transformation overtakes
their entire tyrrhenian fleet:
each alcoholic fights to keep his human form afloat:
the seas fuse nose and mouth into rostrum
with no last words. backs sprout dorsal fins,
hands melt into new, smooth flesh,
surrendering swords. those with growing tails lament
missing feet. they're led to the surface
by a nereid ilithyia for their first breath.
but there is brilliance and mercy in their fate.
the miraculous alcoholics are truly most miraculous
when they slowly metamorphose into dolphins.
they travel beyond death.
why not envy their mutability,
the marvels of their resplendent skin,
and celebrate their ecstasy and suffering,

revel in their ability to subvert all limits,
for when they swim, they take on another form:
they become graceful new animals,
the glint and shadow of their bodies
glide, leaping over the sea, then beneath
the whitecaps, *hinthai*, as the etruscans say,
speeding with the wind,
freed from every bad deed,
like the souls of the ancestors,
free from human misery....

when the miraculous alcoholics throw a party

it will be a wild, fright-inducing night
where the living share their bottles with the dead.
it's not a party unless it scares you.
the costumed guest who truly is a maenad
smiles, slips you deliriants, and dares you
to consume them. soon you will be
holding hands with blindmen
who limbo on the ledge of a skyscraper.
your world will burst like a grapeskin.
you will chase a staring madman
who runs through crowds with a sword
but will realize too late that you are that staring madman.
dionysus will ride in on a lion.
you and he will agree you are a hyena
because you can't stop laughing like one.
you will beg your best friend to put away the gun
and drive you to the hospital,
but he will laugh and abandon you just for fun
on a street in the city's combat zone.
bad news: you threw up on a gangbanger's shoes.
good news: the miraculous alcoholics
send a neon stolen police car to rescue you.
get in, the driver says. *the party is just starting.*
the stare the driver gives as he turns into a satyr says
don't try to hide from the unbridled wild time,
for this night has no master.
this is the sublime thrillride of pleasure and disaster.
it is a night of endless desires.
it is as sure a rite as the stars
and their black sky of burning fires.

the miraculous alcoholics retrieve last evening piece by piece

like scarecrows who scattered their clothes.
awakening naked, face down in a hayfield.
mouthful of drought. head a grab bag
of haggard fragments. see breezy shirtsleeves
search silver birch, openly solicit birds
to nest within patched elbow holes,
as dungarees hang upside down from steeples.
wallet awol. keyring a noose of goose egg.
pajamas, badly damaged phantoms
in the brambles. windsocks stolen
from a rural airport their sole foothold on clothing.
languid, they move ashamedly sideways,
surveying the periphery: one boot on the roof;
another, halfway down a laundry chute.
someone show them how mown down
and windblown souls slowly compose
their disheveled selves, gather their wits,
and bit by bit, their whereabouts
the night before, their wayward wardrobe.

the miraculous alcoholics liquefy their lives

breezing into shebeenfuls of drowned ophelias,
they sleuth secluded booths
where the Moirae plot their mortal stories.
they mean to thieve the very sheen,
the stars and fizz of spirit's gleam,
sneaking up on the three fates with supersoakers
loaded with tequila. *we must be fluid, shifting streams,
not dry, finite threads!* they cry, firing until dead
spindles drip with liquid lives.
cuervo inundates the grimace of klothos the spinner
until she feels fine in all fifty states
and embroiders shining highs in all our days,
so bright with life they can't be switched by dimmers.
the miraculous alcoholics flail away with free cocktails for all
with the bubblebursting breaststroke
of failed beginner swimmers, mustering such gusto
the measurer, lachesis, lengthens all our lives.
happy hours flower and drams dismantle stammer into banter:
boysenberry kamikazes. alabama slammers.
atropos, who always cuts it short, has such a blast
she has to stay all night. all toast the glowing present,
hazy pasts, and suture surer futures: *here
we'll recreate fate and doom into the finest instants!*
as odysseuses finally home under a full moon,
like inmates just let go, they barge right into
fortune's maelstrom like miracles a-spin.
o tilt-a-whirling waterholes where
our heroes give sobriety the old heave-ho.

Matt Schumacher

"a vast sea where there is nothing but the abode of monsters"

<small>phrase from Matthew Paris's *Map of Britain*, 1250</small>

we really get into the swig of things.
call us the miraculous alcoholics.
we're rogue waves. we tip brigs. & our drinking tilts this planet,
blurs all borders, pours forth fitful spirits from its orbits.
gorgonized by porter dense as loch ness
at ancient maps' four corners, we dump jugs
whose currents keep these oceans circumfluent.
icthyocentaurs cavort with our self-portraits.
we'll deal with the old man of the sea
on the carta marina of olaus magnus,
and he'll agree to keelhaul this bar,
which has no business being closed at such an early hour.
proteus will see to it that the bar reopens
as a chain of offshore islands.
o our revelry is so pronounced,
do not doubt that barmen will sight spouters,
colossal, seahorse-headed whales who spit torrents,
who swallow ships upon medieval swedish maps.
these great sea beasts will hurl surly bouncers
from the bar's whereabouts. don't come too close
or our toasts may consume you like jonah:
drought be damned! we drench the thirst-crazed,
desiccated plains of mortal throats with burning rain,
restore the arid dustbowls of the human soul.
as thales claimed all this must be water,
this world's our liquid wonderland.

favorite maritime drinking songs of the miraculous alcoholics

lost at sea

they accidentally drink the ship in a bottle
but one bad omen in miniature
can't sink such plucky drunks:
why, they've swallowed flying dutchmen,
quaffed draughts of stout
washed down with aftertaste of dross,
killed off shipwreck backwash,
finished drinks tainted with splintered
gangplanks and peg legs,
mistakenly helped themselves
to red tide and sea urchin spine,
swilled rimes of ancient mariners.
they've engulfed coast guard
as well as coastal town
as they gulp down breaker and gull cry,
swig sultry multitudes of spirits.
they've dived for beers in quarries like great whites
just as deep sea divers fall backward off boats
and peer down their throats
for sunken floridian hulks, barnacled hulls,
and lost bowsprits. dauntless sailors
must ignore foghorns in unexplored regions
known as the cape of their gaping maws
when steering due south. in dark bars,
they'd like to aim loutish lighthouse lamps
at every oblivious waitress. foam rages in sea caves
just as slurred words set sail in their mouths.

Matt Schumacher

asked why they drink every drink in sight, they reply

the sea monster bestiary
alive inside us multiplies our thirst.
we drink to expand and deepen its great depths,
to send ice floes down its hydrothermal vents.
we drink for loch ness beasts who must dive
steeply to conceal snaky necks,
to help behemoths slip into unfathomable crevasse.
we hammer beers to honor stranded siren songs,
to appease scylla, whose shrieking heads implore
us to complete these alcoholic odysseys.
we tip treacles to right epic wrongs.
we sip for charybdises whose whirlpools
spin and flip us like shipwrecks.
we drink for dejected feejee mermaids,
who swallow hard to forget their ugliness.
we pour down more for stolen narwhal horn
and unborn unicorn, one bloody rip per tentacle
of vampire squid, one damn dram of beer
for coelacanth to dignify each year
they've worn their grizzled fins.
we swallow for swallowed whales within
who wish to swish and thrash their tails.
we drink to lubricate shark and barracuda tooth,
to aid the grace of devil ray and jellyfish.

they tip over niagara falls

the miraculous alcoholics knock back a few.
then these lushes swear a past jag spilled
so far downhill niagara fell. lucky they knew
how to withstand the dumbest drunk stunts,
how to bask in whiskey cask
and barrelroll beer kegs like lumberjacks,
to outlast and master vast cataract,
all while taking in that suicidal view.
shot or spat out of jar or vat,
dumped, stumbling, from dark bar

into sharp daylight, swerving, yet served straight
or on the rocks over horseshoe falls,
they insist upon tipping their waitress, the maid of the mist,
mid-descent, and muse upon impending death
or honeymoons. unidentified survivors
unhinged at the edge, they brag that,
half in the bag, they tipped niagara back
into waterfall while drunk—then swandived
off the fresh ledge of binge. they gasped in freefall,
sipped whitecaps, slipped away
from fatal cliffs when sunk, drank flurries of currents
which hurried to gulp them down whole.
they stole back breath, mulekicked the undertow,
and, like a shot, swallowed their lost souls.

Matt Schumacher

they breach lake okeechobee

when you think they may just sink
they drink swamp things
and accidentally drain the everglades,
exposing crocodile white bellies
and mangrove roots.
even hemingway's keys
may have been moved
to zydeco accordionly the way they
miraculously kayak drained shallows
of sandfly island, and okefonokee,
wallow like walruses in residual lagoons.
yet to honor the calusa
they replace every drop
of sawgrass marsh water
lest one cypress die too dry,
so bullfrogs again begin throat-singing.
drinking money ostensibly whisked away,
heads hungover and ringing, sold bad swampland
in the ten thousand islands
by shysters in barroom booths,
they prove to slyly buy unknown paradise.
these risky kings kick back to sip
ponce de leon's floridian
lost fountain of youth.

a flaskful of inebriated magistrates

the miraculous alcoholics abhor liquor store clerks
who fail to kneel and worship them
as martyrs to some motley cause.
they like all-night vigils of swill
and usurp jerks who lurk in bars.
they throw down jagermeister shots
with inadmissibly asinine anise grins, swallow
until their world twirls and spins
with worlds of drunken miracles,
convened in throats embossed with cuervo gold.
they legislate dictums and writs
to get smashed out of their wits.
like spooked, unsold, and roughshod horses
they hoof and prod waitresses
for martinis with odd names:
houdini chinese water torture clause.
ferae naturae poured in a glass of fate.
proof of evidently neverending bender.
they wait for bartenders to shower them
paid by the hour for their charms
with free drinks and applause.
give them pens so they'll scrawl laws,
treaties entitling citizens to the royalty of open bars.
they promise to leave
restroom stalls leaping with graffiti.

they steer ghost ships into watering holes

yo ho ho and a bottle of rum!
—pirate drinking song

the miraculous alcoholics frolic
in uncharted tavern waters. grabbing taps,
they captain perfect frigates into beer gardens
until the parking lot sits full of spectral hull and sail:
the marlbourough, the san christobal, the florence edgett,
and more. bartender, patron, and waitress barricade the liquor,
ready to bail. blackbeard disembarks
the queen anne's revenge to slake
his outrageous thirst, pouring whiskey down
his severed head's frown, lit sparklers twisted in his hair.
here's captain kidd, playing the part of parched privateer.
it's scary how beer and ordinary grog,
in a dead pirate's eye, glow like ambrosia.
this raised cutlass means soon all will raise a glass on the house,
one rogue shouts. when they do, the bar transforms into a ship
of wayfarers bound for mare incognita. smoke or fog accrues.
scuttlebutt roosts with mutiny. unpatched picaroon
eyes scour barroom booths for loot.
less greedy lafittes teach barflies sea shanties.
at close, the whole pub tips up, half-sunken,
shipwrecked swiftly as a drunk buccaneer,
on halloween, trips over a smashed pumpkin.

favorite maritime drinking songs of the miraculous alcoholics

they drink spring's return

the force that through the green fuse drives the flower
   —Dylan Thomas

they swirl winter's shattered last gasps,
swallow rhododendron and magnolia
from spring's single shockingly sunlit shot glass.
as the lord of the wild beasts pours them the forest,
they match each fresh bud with rushing suds,
and reel, green as seedlings.
they fix the mixed drink equivalent
of a swallowtail butterfly blowing up its wings
and suck from a straw sleek
as the bee hummingbird's beak.
they sip april's streams and may's deepening creeks,
nourish their blood with flash floods,
endure the worst storms of march
with mere cocktail umbrellas.
they drink the glint of the blue giant hyacinth,
snowdrop and striped crocus, avalanche lily.
consuming cloudless, azure skies
effused with bluebird plumage,
relaxed as fixtures at the source of elixirs
which would rightly fill the hugest red tulips
were spring to serve its wildflowered meadows as liquid,
they pour forth its gushing rush of life force,
pitcher after pitcher.

afterworlds

As the only Greek god endowed with the power of māyā ("magic"), Dionysus transcends all forms and evades all definitions; he assumes all aspects without confining himself to any one. By suddenly appearing among men, he introduces the supernatural in the midst of the natural and unites heaven and earth. Young and old, wild and civilized, near and far, beyond and here-below are joined in him and by him. Even more, he abolishes the distance that separates the gods from men and men from animals.

—Jean-Pierre Vernant

the miraculous alcoholics free all the world behind bars

flashing flagrant fake IDs,
they pass for lesser gods in bars
exclusively for deities.
with thirsts like convicts just escaped from jail,
they drink six continents
and most of australia under the table.
sea level's obviously bedeviled
and maps left daft, cartography
bereft of meaning. the known world,
no longer moored to shore,
loses its borders. it floats away,
in fact, while waiting
for the close of their unreasonable fable.
the miraculous alcoholics,
post-apocalyptic tribe, raise their glasses
over the sunken land masses
gone terra incognita
and squint an eye for dead reckoning.
let there be no more jailers! they decry.
such cajolings conjure horses
long ago thrown overboard
in horse latitudes by spanish sailors.
they mount these mythic, spectral steeds,
and are more than four gleeful, anarchic horsemen,
riding off, decolonized and free,
to sink the sunset into fiery, lacustrine waters.

the miraculous alcoholics leap into the past to shoot free pool

as seraphs heavensent,
or suicidal, aloof fools,
they dry dive from dive barstools
onto pool tables. green felt melts,
at their fingertips, into crème de menthe.
blood alcohol count close to death,
their drunken shouts resound
as alcoholic mouth-to-mouth: their larks rescue
former losers, shark toothmarks
and all, from tables' depths.
these poor players, trawled from liquid past, inept
and sprawled onto solid barroom floor,
rest pale as the cue ball, smacked around,
snookered, and almost racked,
but restored again for more.
when resuscitated pool hall losers
cough up eight balls, solids, stripes,
it's like a heimlich's been performed
upon a guilty, famished minnesota fats.
once revived, they buy two drinks
for every boozy guest.
our drinkers pocket pool hall miracles:
the great store of quarters drunks forget,
the sunken treasures of lost bets.

they sip mesopotamian epics

shiduri, divine alewife, serves ethereal beer
at the tavern which rests between life and death.
seeing both living and dead breeze through these doors,
they lure gilgamesh into a bet:
if they can outdrink the assyrian king,
the gods must restore the primordial world.
the famed monarch embarks. his first sip sucks in rivers and creeks.
half out of fear, the miraculous alcoholics take a breath
then swallow the great deep. gilgamesh feels disbelief.
he pounds down rainclouds, gulps the gods' great tears.
the miraculous alcoholics tip the ark like a glass
and chug the primeval flood. utnapishtim laughs on dry land
as the king surpassing all kings passes out and sleeps.
our drinkers bask in liquid victory.
as hungover as those just deposed or usurped,
the dazed ruler of uruk awakens the next day,
sets sail beyond all ends with his new friends:
the stone boatmen row them across the waters of death.
the scorpion people show them the tunnel to the gods,
who let them view space and time be remade.
the miraculous alcoholics stride through
the pristine cedar forest at sunrise,
drinking in the new world,
enkidu, humbaba, and the bull of heaven at their side.

the miraculous alcoholics steal ideal sweetness

> *free, back*
> *into the green,*
> *rich, dapple-*
> *shadowed tresses of the*
> *forest ...*
>
> —Euripides, The Bacchae

they're bees staggering out of the peonies.
fading bodies leave them
ideal thieves to steal honey yet undreamed of,
sweetness unexceeded, from undomesticated species
before kouryete keepers. melisseus can't see them.
the cave's glow overflows, dusk's perfect, dripping gold,
divine honey honoring the god born here long ago.
as shades dyed red, the hue invisible to bees,
they succeed, eluding stings, unlike beebruised cupid.
these honey thieves need no pity:
their tread as light as the egyptian dead's,
weaving between hive and lightning city,
buoyant voyants who dare
to chair promethean committees.
see them stumble like black bears, sweetly stupid.
with aplomb, they reap the dreamy, syruped comb.
replenished from dark recesses, nectar-headed like Makris,
they're slung with mugs of gleaming mead,
free amidst the forest's dapple-shadowed tresses.
and so our lotus-eaters woke with modus and lost will
seeking sweetest substances, chasing katabasis,
because they're obviously reborn immortals.
it's impossible to kill their buzz.

favorite maritime drinking songs of the miraculous alcoholics

they go drinking with villon

*He took a long swig of dead black wine
And he made his way out of this world.*

—François Villon

they decide to try villon's dead black wine
and make their way out of this world.
able to sneak chablis past mephistopheles,

they wish to pour the vagabond parisian poet-thief
a chilled glass of grand cru in the middle of hell.
they audaciously raid hades' underground reserves,

hold their breath in the waters of lethe,
execute a dead man's float upon the river styx.
they burst through purgatory's swinging doors

and shout *i'm buying every last lost soul a fresh drink!*
their ramshackle truck swerves from visibility,
turns downhill on that rutted gouge of a road to the worst,

and delivers free sweet stout to the netherworld.
they soon have all of hell singing
ninety nine bottles of beer on the wall.

finally, they find villon, tell him the living still read his will.
Prince Jesus, crush those bastards!
he shouts. and drinks his fill.

Matt Schumacher

with a hellish splash

the miraculous alcoholics, liquid exorcists,
armed with forty raining days and nights of noah's ark,
flood hades with waterslides, hell yes they do,
until the stark, fiery thereafter
transforms into adventure waterpark.
drooping souls do superloops through rivers of woe.
tantalus tantalizes us so as he glides by
on flumed and chuted ride,
waving with champagne glass in hand. charon merely rows
formerly tormented souls to frivolity.
the dead take a deep breath
then cannnonball into lethe.
hades must admit the melting ski resort theme
at hell's furthest outskirts is a slick, flames-licking touch.
the miraculous alcoholics can't help slipping down
dripping mountainsides just for fun, and very much
like to pretend they're drunken ski instructors
slaloming uncontrollably through hell.
weary, they stay deeply asleep, trapped
in avalanche: tucked away in fake snowbound château,
lost household which continually slides downhill.

their legend grows as they cultivate bliss

the miraculous alcoholics tend elysian fields.
their favorite crops, slow wormwood, sleepy poppy,
ololiuqui and its dreamy soliloquy,
release bliss like sweet red juice
from bitten pomegranate seeds.
departing paradise despite heroic pleas,
they take to the waves,
reap sea beds clean of intoxicating yields:
they sip spindrift mist's aperitif,
imbibe burgundy's red tides,
drain mermaid spray, distill
and bottle sirensongs.
ashore, these wayward sailors
disappear from temperate ships,
but nothing's wrong: they've escaped
to sample wisps of sea in andalusian manzanilla
on the island of the blessed,
to taste test the best breweries' tulips,
those faint notes of grapefruit, juniper, and rhubarb.
wherever stills drip, they're still ripped.
their shaky strides tour taverns far and wide
as prized grand master beer gardeners.

Matt Schumacher

liquid mountaineers

> *The autumn night is vaporless on the lake.*
> *The swelling tide could bear us on to the sky.*
> *Come, let us take the moonlight for our guide,*
> *we'll sail away and drink where the white clouds are!*
>
> —Li Po

astride golden mountainsides,
they elude gravity in hiking boots.
soaked to the socks with halcyon malt
and mount hood hops,
they defy fluid dynamics,
bounding on liquid clouds.
effervescent as pineapple lambics,
they glissade up pale ale trails,
roam meadows of foam.
following in vintner's
grape-stomping footsteps,
eclipsing tipsy sherpa's paths,
they zigzag up switchbacks like drunk yaks
to summit vast shastas.
they enjoy the olympian view
from the vaunted everest of brew
they've managed to consume.
these idlers lean over the valley,
laugh like li po
over the land below,
listen to elation echo.

favorite maritime drinking songs of the miraculous alcoholics

lightning bottleworks

It's like someone spilled a beer all over the atmosphere.
    —Jens Lekman

after they spilled their beers all over the atmosphere,
human eyes imbibed the northern lights.
for more fireworks, step inside. see bolts briefly light
on bottle lips, slender bottle necks and throats that
nearly melt as lightning fights to fit
itself within enclosed glass slopes.
one tourguide nearly died
when he pried open the right bottle of liquified
heat lightning retrieved from past summer evenings.
one wrong drop of electrified lake and sky,
lit up at the same time last spring for miles,
may be fatal. you may be traceable to outer space
or victim to electroshock if you try a type
of upper-atmospheric flash
weathermen name elves and sprites,
previously glimpsed only by pilots.

survive, and you'll be everlastingly revived,
yet shaken by the aftertaste,
your body ablaze with carbonation.
when pouring flying fire in a bottle,
please be advised to pause
lest quicksilver strike fast turn you to fulgurite.
you may need to hide from the unfolding sublime
as thunderheads once piled up miles high
foam and roll in your glass
like vapor lionesses.

Matt Schumacher

they plunder wonderland

glorious as ostrogoths invading gaul,
dismayed by cocktails far too small,
they steal the fabled bottle labeled DRINK ME
and shrink until their drinks loom ten feet tall.
batty as mad hatters, unfolding scaffold,
hoisting ladders, they dowse with stilt-sized straws
a smoke-ring milieu exuded by a blue,
hookah-puffing caterpillar, supine guide
enthroned upon an amanita mushroom.
the kaleidoscopic first sip flips their skating rink
upside-down. think of shattered newton's laws.
their hands grown into toe-tufted, giant panda paws.
falling into glasses, they face mescaline-laced,
shifting time-space continuums,
traced by the pocket watch of the white rabbit.
they bow to, but elude two rumbustious bullies,
inebriated tweedledee and tweedledum,
like evil twins born amidst bad habits,
steer clear of seas of tears and magnifying fears
through escape routes lucid only in minutiae.
from heartless queens shouting *off with their heads!*
and multiplying giantess alices, chasing
runaway narratives, the miraculous alcoholics
steal their ideal tea from the party:
the endlessly replenished beverage,
cordial which gives their cheshire cat grins leverage
in this diminishing miniature
cosmos. opening wide, they dump it down
those rabbitholes so wont to spout nonsense, their mouths.

the miraculous alcoholics mix the apocalypse

bartenders, extravagant braggarts
who claim they can make any drink imaginable:
they pour our future into a glass,
place it before us like fate,
alongside a chaser of the past.
they blend space and time,
send our world spinning. they add
a dash of love, a pinch of hate.
shaken and stirred,
we refuse to believe
until we see them blend
a drink called *the end of the world*
from the far end of the bar.
it looks terrible even from there:
far worse than scary or unfair.
a world of troubled tomato juice and booze on the rocks,
blending ruin, human error, gin, and abuse.
bloody mary in a fight with bloody tom, dick, and harry.
these barkeeps smile their finest armageddon smile.
their free cocktail sits there the rest of the night
like a belligerent punk looking to pick a fight.
not one drunk dares to sit down in front of it.
when they dump it out at closing time
they contend they saved the world.

Matt Schumacher

with a universe of galaxies all elixirs

they'd ride widening gyres,
revolve in whirlpool and spiral, however dire.
blasted as rocketships,
sportive in vortex,
they'd drink dark energy
and slam down the white of the spinning moon,
bloom into vacuum, sublime
on the brink of explosion, like supernova.
they'd drink enigma
and nebula. they'd sip implosion.
they'd drink from big dipper
and drink the whole zodiac,
drink the yawn and hiss
of sun and moon caving in,
of comet trail, of planet
and meteor forming,
drink bloodred jovian storm
and saturnalian ring,
drink time and space
from black holes,
drink singularity
from the unknown's jaws
with impossible straws,
drink big bang and pre-existing abyss,
then drink the universe back into place.

sea reverie

> *the whitemaned seahorses, champing*
> *brightwindbridled, the steeds of mananaan.*
> —James Joyce

drowned, they wonder
what it might be like to be miraculous,
like a starry nightsky sighted in the eye of a hurricane,
to ride the brightwindbridled steeds of mananaan
and grasp the reigns of whitemaned seahorses,
to be chained to gale and squall,
to be a vessel held suddenly by unseen tentacles,
to be all the ocean putting on its cloak of mist,
to nest in estuary, listless with isthmus,
to escape desperate straits with a sail
made of the cape's last whitecaps.

epilogue

they say you must gaze from a glacier
through a great pair of binoculars
or focus palomar's telescopes
to merely glimpse a tempestuous wisp
of the miraculous alcoholics.
some think drink left them as extinct
as sabertooth or mammoth.
others say maybe they mastered warp speed,
and bent time and space to their needs,
or redispersed as liquid,
seeping into streams of ideas.
or rode some huge ice scoop or tequila luge
to eternity's martini.
or surfed the pores and arteries
of the fabulous beast we call being.
rumored to be born again like frogmen
surfacing far from earth
in europa's frozen oceans,
choosing to becloud their heads
with true cumulus, gentler than pillow or bed,
requesting more celestial refreshment
from the wind, that thin, shifty barman,
it may be they are drinking beers which foam over
to form the clouds of our blue sky,
beers ostensibly the size of mountain basins.
light-minded, like a lake poet drifting by,
icing drinks down as if forever leaving town,
but turning one last ear to eavesdrop
as bars and beehives hum their drunken epic,
they leave us signs from a utopian haven:
lines composed smoothly as cumulonimbus.

favorite maritime drinking songs of the miraculous alcoholics

alpenglow's slow, fading eclogues.
liquid's endless effervescence and allure.
falling stars breaking apart in a burst.
all of this as if to say *please don't miss us.*
the miraculous alcoholics are strong and magical creatures.
our playground is the universe.

Notes

"they caper like the satyrs" and "song of satyrnalian mirth": In his book *Dionysos at Large*, Belgian historian Marcel Detienne identifies several trademark dionysian movements. These include swinging, falling, leaping, and stepping forward into revelry with one's right foot raised.

"when they throw a party": In traditional mythical narrative, Dionysus introduces himself memorably; accompanied by a nomadic entourage of spirited revelers, he creates a frenzied commotion of uninhibited drinking, music, and dancing which openly invites all in the vicinity to join. His retinue includes nymphs, satyrs, sileni, and maenads. Theorists speculate that the deity and belief system originated in Thrace. An ecstatic missionary religion, Dionysian ritual and worship swept into Greece and Rome and soon captivated the populace.

"like bold, luckless etruscan pirates": Ezra Pound frequently refers to Dionysus in his Cantos, particularly Cantos II and XVII. Characteristically, dithyrambs were poems of praise for Dionysus and played a grand part at the Dionysia festival. This modern dithyramb revisits a tale told in Ovid's *Metamorphoses* and other ancient sources, a legend which recounts a transformative encounter between the boyish Dionysus and Etruscan pirates.

"they sip mesopotamian epics": The drinking contest imagined herein assumes some familiarity with the oldest known work of literature in the world, *The Epic of Gilgamesh*, which hails from approximately 3000 B.C. Several characters appear from that text: Shiduri, the tavernkeeper at the end of the world; Utnapushtim, the immortal Sumerian Noah; Gilgamesh, king of Uruk; and Enkidu, the epic's wild man who befriends the king, helps him find humility, and ultimately helps him become a more grateful and compassionate human being.

"they steal ideal sweetness": During *Dionysos: Archetypal Image of Indestructible Life*, Carl Kerényi considers an ancient mythos: a group of thieves attempts to raid the sacred cave of Zeus' birth in order to abscond with divine honey. These thieves, trespassing sacrilegiously, glimpse the swaddling clothes of the infant Zeus and must suffer for their transgression: the honey thieves are subsequently transformed to birds. Honey persists in the Dionysian cosmos and is elsewhere a potent mythical symbol. More than one version of myth holds that Makris, a honey-nymph, nurses Dionysus with honey in a cave on the island of Euboia after Hermes rescues him from the Titans. Honey applied to the lips often means the lucky recipient will possess the gift of eloquence. In Egyptian ritual, honey accompanied the dead, and bees were considered tears of their sun god, Ra.

"they go drinking with villon": The quoted material in the epigraph and penultimate line belongs to François Villon. Both passages hail from his poem collection *The Testament*.

acknowledgments

grateful acknowledgment is due these magazines and journals, where the following poems first appeared:

Anti-: "a drunk driving lesson from the miraculous alcoholics"
    "the festive pastimes of the miraculous alcoholics"

Atlanta Review: "they drink spring's return"

basalt: "their legend grows as they cultivate bliss"

Bayou: "sea reverie"

Belleville Park Pages: "the miraculous alcoholics free all the world behind bars"

Chattahoochee Review: "with a hellish splash"

Cimarron Review: "the miraculous alcoholics leap into the past to shoot free pool"
    "the miraculous alcoholics mix the apocalypse"

Cincinnati Review: "a dionysian outburst"

Confrontation: "they go drinking with villon"
    "cocktails crow like roosters"

Diode: "a great deal of kicking up one's heels"
    "song of satyrnalian mirth"
    "perilously liquified in so liquid an era"
    "miracle everglades"
    "with a universe of galaxies all elixir"

The Feathertale Review: "they revive dead rivertowns"
    "incomprehensibly thirsty"

The Fiddlehead: "lost at sea"

Fourteen Hills: "les alcooliques miraculeux et le bateau ivre"

Green Mountains Review: "miraculous backwards abecedarius recited for police"

      "asked why they drink every drink in sight, they reply"
      "a thirst as legendary as their exploits"
      "they steer ghost ships into watering holes"

Gris-Gris: "liquid mountaineers"
      "they sip mesopotamian epics"

The Kerf: "drinking song for loaded poets"

Muse/A: "when the miraculous alcoholics throw a party"

North American Review: "a flaskful of inebriated magistrates"

PacificREVIEW: "lightning bottleworks"

Painted Bride Quarterly: "drinking song"
    "the miraculous alcoholics drink the great lakes"

Permafrost: "drunken coronation"

Redivider: "the miraculous alcoholics look sleek and composed"

Rougarou: "should auld acquaintance be forgot"

Skidrow Penthouse: "the kings of spilled drinks"

SubTerrain: "their tossing ships"
    "miraculous backwards abecedarius recited for police"

Vallum: "non-anonymously, the miraculous alcoholics unanimously"

Western Humanities Review: "they caper like the satyrs"
    "the miraculous alcoholics retrieve last evening piece by piece"

Witness: "why they drink deep"

about the author

When not composing fantastical drinking songs, **MATT SCHUMACHER** will very likely be found teaching higher ed English and Humanities courses, hanging with his better half, Kaley, or circuitously sauntering through the Kenton neighborhood of Portland, Oregon, exercising two rambunctious rescue shelter pups. Editor of the New Fabulist journal *Phantom Drift*, the author has published some eight poetry collections, including his first book, *Spilling the Moon*; the incendiary riffs of *The Fire Diaries*; the Western place and persona poetry of *Ghost Town Odes*; a surrealistic almanac written to celebrate nature and animals, *Mooncalf Almanac*; and a prose-poem chapbook featuring a time-traveling Thomas De Quincey, *A Missing Suspiria de Profundis*.

Of unknown, but possibly inebriated origin.

www.ingramcontent.com/pod-product-compliance
Lightning Source LLC
LaVergne TN
LVHW091315080426
835510LV00007B/505